THE RETAIL LIFE: A STORE MANAGER'S COMPANION

THE RETAIL LIFE: A STORE MANAGER'S COMPANION

Tierney Alexander

Writers Club Press
San Jose New York Lincoln Shanghai

The Retail Life: A Store Manager's Companion

Writers Club Press
an imprint of iUniverse, Inc.

For information address:
iUniverse, Inc.
5220 S. 16th St., Suite 200
Lincoln, NE 68512
www.iuniverse.com

You say you want a career in Retail—Are you nuts?!!

ISBN: 0-595-22496-2

Printed in the United States of America

INTRODUCTION

I'm not really sure as to why I decided to write this book. Actually, it all started as a few scribblings of my experiences as a Retail manager; sometimes the days were so tough that I just had to write down my feelings to try and make sense of it all. Before I knew it, I had 15 chapters! And I knew that if I felt this way about my life in retail that surely there were other people out there who could relate. I think retail people are among the most misunderstood folks in the world!! Actually, I'm not sure there are people out there who actively *try* to understand us! Shoppers as a whole don't see us as real people, we're just the drones who are never around to help them get the item off the top shelf; folks who work in the corporate arena have no idea the complexity of the work we do; even our bosses have forgotten—or never knew in the first place—what it takes to survive just one day in a store. It all sounds pretty negative and believe me, I'll be the first to admit that there have been more than a few times I've scratched my head in wonder as to why I continue to stay in this field. But, the more I thought about the feelings I was putting down on paper, the more I realized that probably every other Retail manager out there has experienced something similar, and that it might be fun to share. So many times I've felt that I was the only one going through all these things and how nice it would have been to pick up a little book like this and see that retail problems are universal to all retail establishments. I think in times of despair that it might have given me the strength to go on. So…for all you new Retailers out there, and for my wizened colleagues who might just get a chuckle out of it, I offer this little tome.

You and I both know that aside from ourselves and our families—who witness our travails—there is really no one out there who understands what we go through. I think my real hope is that my fellow retail professionals might read this book and turn up a knowing smile, because what I know you will find are stories that relate to your own experiences in this crazy world—experiences which would greatly challenge the average person with no retail background. And, I'm hoping that in some way my friends, that you will feel what I have to remind myself every day…that if you can make it in retail, you can make it *anywhere*, because there is no profession out there that expects as much.

Chapter 1—Frame of Reference

I am coming from over 18 years experience in the retail field. I've worked big boxes and small boxes, I've managed multiple small units, budgeted, hired, fired, trained and analyzed P&L's. While I have worked with hourly associates, and was one for a short time, I am using my experiences as a Retail manager as the basis for this book.

Where to start? Well, how I got into retail might be a good place. Now, some of you may have worked your way up from cashier or stock person, but I did not do it that way. Although, let me say here that I certainly admire those of you who did that and make no mistake, you folks know more about retail and can get a store through the roughest times ten times better than any inexperienced manager hired from the outside! Having said that, may I introduce myself as one of those managers who came in from the outside! The only thing I can say in my defense is that I was brought in at the store level and to survive in that atmosphere you have to learn quickly! I don't plan on divulging any information on the names of the companies I've worked for—you know how everything in retail has to be so hush-hush—but I will say that I have worked for some of the giants of the business and feel my experiences will be familiar to anyone who has worked in the retail field, despite the size of the company.

While I have worked in the corporate setting of retail as well, I've organized this book so that each chapter looks at a different area of the Retail experience at the store level—from a manager's viewpoint. The corporate side is too like corporate life in any industry, whereas the culture at the store level is a wacky world in and of itself. From time to time the manager's viewpoint I relate may be similar to that of an hourly associate, but I can only profess to know how I personally felt about the situation. Besides, some aspiring hourly associate can write his own book! I suppose I should also say that this book is not for upper-level Retail managers—they probably won't take too kindly to some of the sentiments I've expressed in the following pages. Oh well, if they feel too badly about it, they can always take a look at their paycheck—it's a heck of a lot higher than mine or yours!! Enjoy the book!

Chapter 2—The Manager's Schedule

Could much of anything be worse than retail hours? Well, I guess a lot of things could be, but it sure doesn't seem that way when you first look at next week's schedule! Now, some store managers are able to garner a routine schedule of sorts, say, the same night closing every week and the other four days opening—or a variation. Unfortunately, I have only had this luxury once in my retail career. The other 17 years have seen me working the strangest combination of hours: 8AM-5PM on Sunday, 3PM-Midnight on Monday, 10AM-7PM on Tuesday, off Wednesday, 7AM-4PM on Thursday, off Friday, 1PM-10PM on Saturday. And that's just one possible variation! Very rarely do I get two days off in a row. I usually can plan on one weekend off a month, but in order to get that I have to work a tour of 8 days in a row! The worst scenario for any manager is not knowing what you will work *next* week until late *this* week, say Wednesday, for a week that starts on Sunday! Talk about not being able to plan for anything. Unless you make your schedule yourself, or have season tickets to the theater, or a class paid for, and a deal with your boss to get you off in advance, it is certainly difficult to cultivate any type of life outside retail other than going to work and then coming home and collapsing. One area that is really a problem is church attendance; having weekends off is a luxury in this business and it is very difficult to find a retail company that will guarantee you every Sunday or Saturday off. If you do have interests outside work you have to ask way in advance to make sure you aren't scheduled and even then there's always the caveat: "As long as business permits." Folks who work a Monday-Friday job have no concept of this phenomenon: we retail professionals actually have to ask permission in order to do something on our own time! I actually had a high-ranking company official tell me once that a lot of people go into retail because they want that revolving, unpredictable schedule. Now I ask you, who told her that? The Schedule Fairy?!! I suppose there are folks out there, myself included at rare times, who enjoy having some weekdays off for appointments, etc. but I swear I have never talked to one retail management colleague in 20 years who has actually said they enjoyed their schedule!

Chapter 3—Holidaze

"Holiday." This word is defined in the Retail Manager's Dictionary as follows: a non-word; no such thing; are you crazy?! For me, after the unpredictable nature of the schedule, this is the most daunting area of retail management. Almost every retailer is now open on major and minor holidays, which means that those days have now become just another workday for associates and managers alike. New Years Day, Easter, July 4th and a host of others have become possible sales bonanzas for retail corporations. Of course, the irony is that the corporate office employees still get holidays off—with the probable exception of systems help desk professionals—while the stores are fully operational. Even Thanksgiving and Christmas have become fair game. The greatest irony to me is that invariably sales on most major holidays are minimal—imagine that, customers stay home with their families in droves—but the powers that be in retail would rather incur more payroll expense than sales as opposed to being the guy that isn't open. For managers this is the rub: why not let associates spend these special days with their families? Is it any wonder that the family unit is a thing of the past? A great majority of retail and other service associates are forced to work on days that were traditionally times for families to bond and share special memories.

Not only is the actual day in question fragmented for the manager who draws the holiday, but the normally joyous parts of the season leading up to the holiday are also compromised. Take the Christmas holiday for example. Firstly, the Christmas goods start arriving before Halloween; then, the directive from corporate has the Christmas decorations going up before Thanksgiving. Corporate or regional directives for issues like staffing start getting e-mailed in September. Some retailers, under the perfectly logical guise of being totally prepared for the season, have their managers in the field making mock schedules for the weeks between Thanksgiving and Christmas before they've had a chance to breathe after the Back-To-School crush! It's merciless really, and the result is a prolonged angst to the point that managers simply want it all to be over; there is no time or advocation from above to actually enjoy the experience. The season is a melee of frantic phone calls for sales and staffing information, tense managers and associates walking around with furrowed brows and impossible workloads for all those involved.

Forget visiting out-of-town family during any holiday season. For the Christmas season most retailers slap a "black-out" period from mid-November to January 1st where managers are not permitted to ask for any scheduling considerations. Six-day workweeks are the norm—some retailers compensate managers for the extra day, some don't. The same goes for July 15th through September 2nd for Back-To-School. Having family visit during this time is not advisable either as managers are usually dead-on-their-feet and/or pre-occupied. For me, for as long as I can remember, Christmas and Thanksgiving are simply days off; and, I'm one of the lucky ones because the retailers I've worked for have yet to decide to remain open on these days. I'm really too tired and run down to celebrate and for the last few years I haven't even put up decorations. I have great respect for my colleagues—usually the ones with children—who find the energy to decorate their homes and make the time to celebrate with their families.

Beyond all the above, I guess the most mentally frightening thing about being a retail manager during the holiday season is when I realize I am singing the songs from the store's holiday music tape in the shower! Or worse yet, at the store I start humming the *next* song on the tape *before* it actually starts playing! That's pretty pathetic!

You may have similar issues with holidays, or you may be thinking, "this girl has been in retail a little too long!" On that I think I will agree with you, especially after an incident that occurred last year during Christmas. I was the closing manager on a night a week before Christmas. The store was trashed; everyone was tired and just trying to survive the rest of the evening. An hour before close I saw a little girl, perhaps six years old, happily pushing a shopping cart around which she had filled with various items. Every now and then she'd add another item, emulating her parents who were shopping around the corner. Now, please know that I am normally upbeat and very friendly with my customers, but when I looked at that cart, all I could think of was how long it was going to take to put all that stuff back! I marched right up to that little girl, with I'm sure, the most deranged look on my face, and said, "don't put anything else in that cart that you are not planning to buy!" *She was six, for Pete's sake*!! As she ran off, practically in tears, to find her parents, I decided right then and there that it was time for me to start looking for another job. I knew that as a manager, if I could not even pretend to take joy in my customers, that I was certainly not going to be able to lead my associates to a successful selling season. Of course, deciding to get a job outside retail and finding one are two different things, but that's another chapter.

For the rest of this chapter, I need to address an issue that has affected every retail manager I know: sickness during the holiday season! Christmas is the worst, but all holidays suffer from this phenomenon; if it's not a winter cold, it's a summer cold. Strep throat might as well be called the "Retail Disease." Mononucleosis is right up there too. Think about it. You've got people working long physical hours, pressure from above to annihilate last years sales figures, endless battles with cranky customers over price adjustment and return policies, and the work still has to get done even though hourly associate call-offs are at an all-time high. It's the perfect recipe for disaster, and it takes the form of death-ly ill managers. The only problem is, you just can't be sick. There's just too much to do and absolutely no one at corporate or the regional office gives a hoot how you are feeling. And worse yet, even your colleagues at the store can't care because they feel just as bad and can't take off either! Don't expect sympathy or understanding from anyone! It's just nowhere to be found because everyone is too busy dealing with the additional sales and all the tasks that the season brings.

Once during the Christmas holiday I came down with mononucleosis. My doctor told me to take a month off with complete bed rest. When I passed this information on to my boss, his first remark was, "I've never heard of mono." After I explained what it was, he then went on to say that he couldn't possibly afford to have me out that long. Now, I was 23 years old and naïve about my rights, so I agreed to stay out for one week. I did feel a lot better after the week so I went back to work and over the next several weeks eventually got my strength back; but, to this day I get sick every time someone around me gets a sniffle and I swear it is because some damage was done to my immune system during that bout with mono—especially since I was not able to get the full bed rest my doctor prescribed.

Okay, the next example I'm going to give you will also be repeated in the chapter titled: "Stupid things bosses say." It is just so typical that I wanted to include it here as well. One of the reasons I have the time to write this book is because I have been granted a six-week medical leave due to having a hysterectomy. So, thankfully this year I have been home during the entire Christmas holiday season; I haven't made any six-year-olds cry either! At any rate, I did not know originally that I needed such major surgery. All I knew was that starting in July I felt pain in my right side. By October it was much worse and occurring every day; by November it was affecting my ability to do my job, which, as you know—what with erecting shelves and displays and carrying large amounts of clothing, etc.—is very physical. I had an ultrasound, which showed a tumor near my uterus. The doctor scheduled me for surgery December 7th and told me if he simply had to remove the tumor I would be out about two weeks, but that if the tumor was also inside my uterus it would require the more major surgery of a hysterectomy. When I first told my direct superior she was very concerned and told me to do what I had to do; for one whole day, she even grabbed anything she saw me carrying and carried it for me. Then, she was faced with the task of finding managers in the region to help fill the shifts I would miss. Remember, we're talking the Christmas season here; none of her colleagues wanted to help. It actually got pretty ugly with the regional manager having to force other stores to go a little leaner so that our store could be staffed. So, after that first day of sincere concern, my manager slipped to no concern whatsoever; she stayed out of my dealings with corporate on family leave issues and pretty much avoided me for the three weeks before my surgery. I was back to lifting everything necessary, etc. Less than a week before I left the regional manager came for a visit. After spending a lengthy time in the office with my boss the regional sought me out on the floor and said, "I hear you are having some surgery?" I told her that yes, I needed to have a tumor removed. Now here's what she said next: "Yes, that interests me because I wasn't aware that they did that type of surgery this time of year." I swear that's what she said!! Well, I don't know how you would have taken that remark, but I was extremely uncomfortable. She went on to say that she had had the same type of surgery two times before and went in on a Friday and was back to work on Monday, so she couldn't understand why my doctor's prescribed time off was for 2-6 weeks. Now I'm sorry, but this woman runs 18 large stores for my company and her company car is a Lexus!! Even though I knew that she was probably just frustrated because of all the scheduling issues that arose due to my absence, I just couldn't forgive her for her insensitivity. It took me quite a while, in fact, before I could think of her with any respect at all!

I'm sure you have had or heard similar horror stories about being away from the store during the holidays. If you haven't been ill yourself you've surely had to pick up the slack caused when one of your colleagues has been out. In the end, it's just best to stay healthy all year round, or at least have the loyalty to only get sick during non-peak times!

One other thing I must add here concerns my observations of retail goings-on while I have been recuperating. Since I haven't been a part of this stressful holiday season I am remarkably calm. I've actually enjoyed the winter snow and all the holiday shows on TV. On Christmas day I had the fleeting thought that the next day I'd call my store and see how everyone was doing. Then I realized that for me the day after Christmas was just another day, but for my working colleagues it would be a frantic day of merchandise returns!! It suddenly dawned on me just how different this season is for people who are not involved in retail; truly they just couldn't possibly have a clue what it is like!!

Chapter 4—The Joy of Employees

Political correctness dictates calling these folks "associates," a term that was adopted by most retail organizations in the mid-eighties; presumably it sounded "gentler and kinder" than the heretofore used terms of employee, or worse yet, subordinate. At any rate, to a retail manager they represent the ultimate dichotomy: we love them; we hate them! In truth, we live and die by their performance. It is interesting to note here that over the last several years, as the economy shifts to a more technological and service orientation, retail has had to weather a shift in employee availability, and more importantly, employee attitude. In the old days there were plenty of people looking for work, people who were willing to do the necessary tasks for fairly low hourly wages, and who stayed in a job indefinitely. They did what they had to do and respected their superiors because that was what kept them in the job. Nowadays, things are different.

Oh sure, there are still folks out there who have a great work ethic and maintain a high level of performance no matter what their wage—full-time retail associates usually fall into this category, although I've certainly known a few exceptions. For the most part, however, retail, by virtue of the economic need to staff stores with less-expensive associates, is now held prisoner by the many-faceted whims of the part-timer. Part-time associates take many forms. Here are a few you are sure to be familiar with (Note: these categories, in my experience are the rule, but there are always exceptions; please read them with that in mind):

The Multi-job Associate—These folks have a "real" job, perhaps full or part-time, that comes first. Your store is merely a source of additional income or a discount opportunity. During the hiring process they seem so perfect. I mean, wow, they appear so enterprising and organized; most have fairly good education and good interviewing skills, and in truth, they usually are respectful of management and very productive. The downside comes when the "real" job gets crazy, or working two jobs, which seemed like a good idea in the beginning, starts to take a toll on them physically. Can you say "call-off?" Since your store is the second priority call-offs are inevitable. And there's not much notice either; you can usually expect the call right when their shift is supposed to start or a little before, and by then you are already behind, the store is trashed and you are really counting on them being there. So, great contributors when they show up, but don't bet the farm on them being there for every scheduled shift.

The Day-time Mom—Oh, if only they had better availability!! Most can work when their kids are in school—9AM-2PM; heaven forbid Dad watch the kids when he gets home, so don't ever expect to have them in the evening. They are great with customers, have a great work ethic and rarely question management directives! Pretty much their only downside is in regard to their kids. School is closed due to snow; can you say "call-off?" Naturally, that's the day you need them to show up the most because all the other kids that are off school are now coming to your store!! Forget advance notice; if the kid is sick you'll find out when you show up in the morning and Mom isn't there; the same goes for impromptu teacher's meetings. These gals are usually not available for weekends, the entire summer, or holidays—basically your busiest times. This is another group that is great when they show up but they'll let you down when you need them the most.

The Night-time Mom—Same as above in terms of work ethic and productivity. The nice thing they provide is maturity on the floor. Same downside if their kids get sick; Dads can rarely deal with the responsibility so Mom has to call off. If your store does a lot of business in the evenings these call-offs lead to inability to recover the store which sets up for a rough opening the next day.

The Experienced Retail Hopper—These folks have it down to a science. They've worked at every retailer and restaurant around. They say all the right things in the interview, and though you know good and well to be suspicious of all their movement, you need someone bad and this person will be able to hit the floor running without much training; it's like you're in denial during the interview; you convince yourself that they just haven't found the right place and that *you* will surely be able to tame their wanderlust. RIGHT! Here's what happens. They start out great. They pick up the register so fast your head is spinning and, in two days, they are helping you reorganize departments. They are very productive and you actually hear yourself saying things like, "man, if I had 10 more of him/her, I'd have it made." All too soon the honeymoon ends. Maybe they start to slack off a little here and there, although, when you are really desperate they still come through for you. Maybe there starts to be a little more cash shortage in the registers than there was before, but this usually happens when they are training new recruits so the burden of investigation is difficult. Maybe they start to get close to a few vulnerable associates and start to plant seeds of disillusionment regarding certain managers or other associates. Oh, and if you bring them into the office for a counseling session, they are the first ones to threaten calling employee relations because "their rights" are being usurped. Somehow, it all just starts to go south and you are left scratching your head. In hindsight, you pull out their original application and see that they've worked for 5 different retailers or restaurants in the last 16 months, and you vow never to fall for that one again! Until the next time….

The Minor—These youngsters are a necessary evil due to the shrinking labor pool. Some turn out to be great and end up staying with you up to and including their college years. Others just drive you crazy. Of course, there's the added break constraints that cause trouble on any busy day—a required lunch break within 5 hours of clocking in—but probably the scariest thing about this group is…their PARENTS! Now, one given is that Mom or Dad always does the calling off; while a manager might huff and puff to a minor over the phone, what can they do when a parent calls in?

"Thanks Mrs. So and so, tell so and so to get better soon." I've had to get porcelain implants on the bottom of several of my teeth thanks to grinding my way through that statement so many times over the years! All sicknesses aside, there's also the phenomenon of the unplanned family obligation. Suddenly Mom will decide that the child needs to see Aunt Sue over the weekend, or Dad's company gave him tickets to the ball game. It is amazing that the one group of people we managers count on most to instill a good work ethic in their children, usually turn out to be the worst offenders. Naturally, to most parents the priority is schooling and a retail job comes in a distant second when unusual circumstances arise. For instance, the associate went to school today but has a cold; Mom decides that the 5-9PM shift he is scheduled to work at your store tonight is much less important than getting rest so that he can go to school tomorrow, so…call-off. Now, who can argue with that logic, especially if you are a parent yourself? But, as the closing manager, you are livid; there goes recovery, there goes that project you had planned, etc. Other downsides to this group are shortened attention spans, the propensity to travel in packs (the minute you turn your back, they congregate together in one area of the store, preferably far away from the nearest customer they might otherwise be helping), and the lack of "ownership" feelings toward the store or the work they do in it. It is especially difficult to get these folks to actively sell to customers or get remotely excited about a pending visit from company officials. Also expect limited availability; if there is a sport or club out there that requires them to meet on nights or weekends when you need them most, you can bet your minors will join! (Actually, I have found that the kids who are involved in many school activities have the best work ethic; I'm just sore because they are so active I can't schedule them as much as I'd like!). While they could possibly make up the bulk of your associate staff, they can, as a group, be the least productive, which skews the workload unfairly toward your full-timers and other managers.

The Young Adult Who Still Lives With Mom and Dad and Doesn't Really Need the Money but Gets a Job Because That's What Adults Do—You can really say "call-off" this time! This group you just want to strangle! Most of them are highly intelligent and very good workers...that is, when they take the notion to do so. After they've just completed a very detailed merchandising project, and it's just so beautiful you have tears in your eyes, you find yourself saying, "boy, can we make him/her full-time?" Then you remember the other 60%

of the time when they are the worst congregating offenders, or they come in and boldly say, "I just don't feel like helping customers today," usually within earshot of you *and* a customer! What a frustrating group; they call off on a whim, or they'll come in for their shift but let you know they are sick and then ask to leave early, etc. This group is usually very aware of the staffing issues at your store and manage to keep their jobs despite frequent lapses in regard to following policy. Why? Because, when push comes to shove they know how to do everything in the store, and in a crush time you need them to survive!

The Combination—Most associates fall into this category, even managers at times! For the most part they are either great or terrible. Some will be terrific 80% of the time but falter every now and then. Vice versa, some will be totally unproductive 80% of the time, but 20% of the time, usually when you least expect it, they will show flashes of brilliance that makes you wonder what brain cells they are functioning on the rest of the time! At any rate, for the retail manager, this is the group that comprises about 95% of the staff, and it is imperative to get the most out of them on a daily basis.

The Star—This person can come from any of the above groups. It is someone who—barring major catastrophes— is always there for every shift. They come in with a positive attitude and no project is too daunting for them. They supplement management in that they will actually suggest projects that may have slipped the manager on duty's mind. They take pride in the store and will give 110% before an important visit. They'll even spend their own money to help decorate the break room, or use their break time to clean out that disgusting thing that is the staff refrigerator. You can't say enough about them and thank goodness they exist because otherwise the life of a retail manager would be too unbearable to survive. Another nice thing about this group is they genuinely like their managers and will do anything they can to help them. If even 5% of your staff falls in this group right now, consider yourself very lucky!

As I stated before, these groups are large stereotypes and there are always exceptions. One thing that is 100% true these days, though, is that with the shrinking labor pool retailers are having to deal differently with hourly associates than they did, say, 15-20 years ago. Employee Relations is a huge part of every large company and even most small ones, and it is increasingly difficult for managers to have total autonomy in regard to disciplinary action toward non-performers. For example, 18 years ago I ran several convenience stores. One night I was out inspecting one of my units and I noticed my clerk did not have a uniform on; when I asked him why, he said it was dirty. I explained to him that he needed to have his uniform on at all times. He promptly told me he was feeling sick and if I didn't leave him alone he would go home right then and there. I was horrified at his lack of respect and told him that he needn't act that way—I was merely telling him what was required of him. He simply handed me his keys and walked out, right past the line of people who were waiting to buy gas and cigarettes!! It was a good thing I knew how to run the register and close the store! The next morning when he showed up for his shift, again without his uniform, I fired him. Now, if that scenario happened today, I would have to call my boss, who would tell me that in order to fire him we have to get permission from Employee Relations and/or the Legal department and before they can be brought in, I have to show evidence of oral and written counseling sessions documented for the *same* offense? For me as a manager charged with running a business, this changing tide has brought much frustration. Most times I feel my hands are tied, and it certainly makes it harder to wrest a productive performance out of that "combination" group. It also allows non-performers to take up space which could go to people out there who really need and want to work. By far the worst byproduct is that it gives the message to young or new associates that you can get away with disrespect for your managers or lack of work and still keep your job. I know that out of necessity my standards have dropped over the years; as a professional this troubles me greatly, but in order to be successful I have had to change my expectations. How about you?

Chapter 5—Associate Romances

You know, can't those kids just do their work and go home? Sooner or later a couple of them notice each other and fall madly in love! For management, it's just never a good thing. You've got to keep them separated on the floor. Otherwise they'll stare lovingly into each other's eyes and miss every customer who walks by. If you give them their breaks at the same time you've practically got to put a stop watch on them or a fifteen minute break will turn into a half-hour. If one calls off chances are the other will also. Oh, and if there are any out-of-the-way spots in your store, be prepared: you may get an eyeful the next time you walk into the stock room. Better yet, keep the stock room locked.

It's bad enough when they are in love; it's even worse when they break up or have issues in their relationship—and sooner or later they *always* do. If they both stay at the store there's awkwardness for all involved. The other associates don't know whom to support, and tension is very evident when they are both on the premises. As a manager, you can't get involved in the mess without jeopardizing your professionalism. There's a lot of he said/she said going around the breakroom and this can sometimes spill out onto the sales floor.

Of course the problem worsens if you have multiple couples! Obviously some of them act with integrity and decorum but for the most part, they just can't help themselves. Ah, young love!

Chapter 6—Payroll

I suppose this chapter could be summed up in 3 words: There's never enough! However, there are some nuances to this issue that bear discussing. Retailers look at payroll expense in many ways. First and foremost, payroll is the single largest controllable expense and as such can quickly have a huge impact on the bottom line; for this reason payroll is the first luxury cut in times of sales decline or other financial difficulties. And, while cutting hours has little effect on the corporate offices, it can play havoc with a manager's ability to staff the store, the daily operation of the store and the type of workweek the management staff has to endure. Retailers track and set payroll goals a number of ways, most notably by hours used at some average rate per hour, or as a dollar percentage of sales. While some companies have developed complex matrix systems based on selling and task hours during peak and non-peak times, in the end it all comes down to payroll dollars spent. Minimizing payroll expense without harming sales potential probably takes more of a manager's time than anything else, and there's no lack of advice from above. Here are a couple of scenarios:

The Managers Work It Approach: Payroll focus is on hourly expense; manager pay is considered a fixed cost and excluded from daily payroll expense analysis. Since managers cost the same dollar amount whether they work 40 or 100 hours a week, they suddenly become a prime asset when times are bad. So, if it looks like the store is going to come in high on payroll expense as a result of low sales to plan, it behooves the manager to cut hourly shifts and fill in personally. This lowers payroll expense and the manager is a hero...until he explodes as a result of major burnout! Short-term financial gains are offset by high manager turnover and lost sales opportunities. Some companies who seem to advocate this style of operation gain the reputation of being a "churn and burn" employer or "sweatshop."

The All Inclusive Approach: Payroll focus is on total dollars spent to staff the store. In this case the average hourly rate used to plan payroll is skewed because of high per-hour pay for managers. The nice thing about this scenario is that managers are encouraged to work only their scheduled hours; for instance, they can only be put into the system at 40 hours per week; working extra hours does not behoove them. In fact, any time a manager's shift is deleted from the schedule—say, they take a vacation day which rolls into another expense line—payroll expense for the store decreases dramatically in terms of the numbers used for daily analysis. By the same token, in crunch times, up to 3 part-time associates can work a shift for the same cost as one manager. The downside to this scenario is that if managers won't consent to take paid time off, the store must be staffed with less people in order to meet hour allowances and both sales and daily operations suffer.

Help from above comes in many disguises but boils down to one of two: hours are cut or additional hours are available.

Something extraordinary has to happen to bring about the latter. Sales must suddenly balloon to out-of-this-world-higher-than-plan levels. Retailers, smelling even larger windfalls, will usually get the grass roots system in gear immediately and have the field management reassess payroll goals; stores are notified that they can now add a set number of hours to the schedule in order to take advantage of the booming business. As a manager I have always found these calls to be a bittersweet phenomenon. For one, if sales have been that great I'm usually buried under 3 days worth of recovery…and two, I'm already working the staff I have to maximum capacity…and finally three, there's no way I can dig myself out to go about hiring anyone! By the time I could sit down and call everyone on the schedule and beg them to work more, or interview prospective new people, the sales boom is over and I'm back to the lean, mean, payroll machine that I usually have to run. Now, I know that HR managers—you know, the ones who have never worked in the field—advocate that I have good candidates in my back pocket who I can call at a moment's notice. RIGHT! Most folks who don't get hired immediately after they apply usually just go down the street; they certainly don't sit around for weeks on end waiting until I have an opening! In the end, it's almost better to suffer through the good times with the staff on hand, because next week sales will settle down and all the extra hours will be cut.

Cutting payroll hours is a thankless job. Of course no one bears the brunt like the individual store manager. See, corporate and regional operatives have no personal involvement; that particular joy is left up to the poor manager who gets to call the associate and let him know his shift has been cut! In addition to the fact that you have now literally taken money out of that associate's pocket, you also have to deal with reduced staff morale, as well as possible accusations of manager/associate favoritism if the same associates get cut again and again. Moreover, depending on the number of times cuts are made and the severity of each, it is difficult to keep a staff on hand; most associates have bills to pay and want to have a certain amount of hours they can count on each week; otherwise, they quit and go where schedules are more dependable.

By far the worst case of payroll modification I have experienced as a manager has involved a flurry of payroll changes in a short period of time. For instance, payroll for the week is planned several weeks in advance, and the schedule has been finalized and out for at least five days. Then, for some unknown reason, sales don't come anywhere near plan for the first two days of the week. The regional office calls and says to cut hours by 30, so the management staff analyzes the situation and calls several associates. The schedule is reprinted and business goes on as usual. Then, it turns out that the first two days were a fluke and for the next two days sales go through the roof. Because of the cuts, staff on the floor is too lean and all projects fall behind. On Thursday evening, the regional office calls and says that since sales have been so fabulous the store now has an additional 75 hours to spend! This would ordinarily be joyous news, except that all the people who got cut earlier in the week have made plans and are now unavailable! For managers there is such a credibility issue here. First, they call and cut an associate's shifts. Then, they call two days later and ask the associate to not only work the original shifts but also to add as many shifts as they can! If this type of payroll roulette is a common occurrence, it can play havoc on a store's operation, a retailer's reputation with potential associates, and a manager's personal morale.

Suffice it to say that payroll considerations are a bane to a manager's daily existence!

Chapter 7—Merchandising

While there really isn't a right or wrong way to merchandise, there certainly are do's and don'ts to deal with. The challenging thing for managers is that one boss can tell you something looks great, and then his or her boss can come in the same day and tell you it's all wrong! Suffice it to say that help from above almost always results in major floor moves. The main thing is to keep the merchandise neat and the fixtures looking as full as possible.

I once worked with a manager who, on a busy Saturday, had sold most of the merchandise on a main aisle table. She decided to switch the broken item out and fill the table with something she had plenty of stock in. Unfortunately, in the middle of the move, when the table had been emptied but not refilled, business boomed and she got called to the registers to ring for an extended period of time. Even worse, the new regional manager for the store came in for an unannounced visit—her first time ever in the store—and was horrified to see a "prime real estate" fixture empty on a busy Saturday. Even though the situation was explained to her she gave the store's general manager a "below standard" rating for merchandising on her next performance appraisal! I guess the moral of the story is you've always got to have the merchandising in order no matter what is going on. Of course, that's easier said than done.

One thing that irks me is shoddy merchandising. I always tell my associates when I find it that I just know they are deliberately trying to give me chest pains. An example would be empty hat merchandisers; either it's a naked head or a wire grid and without anything on them they just look awful. How about empty sign holders! The same goes for naked mannequins. I swear I never see an associate or customer removing the clothes, but all of a sudden, a previously dressed form is now naked for all the world to see! Or, a rack has been changed to a different item but the body form on top is still dressed in the previous item—this just drives me crazy!! What about empty accessory hooks or face-outs/arms with only one item on them? It's definitely a never-ending battle, and one which a manager cannot win alone. You absolutely have to train the associates to help notice these anomalies or your store will forever look unkempt.

Of course, no one can make a store look worse than that all-important entity—the customer. I've always wondered why, when a stack of t-shirts is perfectly sized, and the customer needs a small, they demolish the entire pile and grab a small from the middle?! Or, they open up every shirt in the size they need and leave them strewn over the top of the entire table?! I know it has something to do with a myth about every garment being different. When I'm feeling really calm and want a laugh I just observe a newly folded table for awhile and watch for the customer shenanigans that will surely ensue: they check to make sure the arms are the same length; they pull and stretch an item's fabric in every conceivable direction; they let several items drop off the table onto the floor without a glance; they leave an item from across the store on top of the table and walk off; they smell the fabric; they hold an item up against them that couldn't possibly fit; they look at an item for prolonged moments, as if hoping it will transform into something else. By far the worse is a customer who watches an associate folding a table and then proceeds to trash it while the poor associate is still standing there! I swear if I ever go into politics I am going to propose a bill that requires anyone who wants to shop must work at least two days in a retail store; I figure two days of recovering the floor will cure them of any propensity to ruin nicely merchandised fixtures while they're shopping. Wouldn't that be great?

I think my favorite time of year is peak time when some retailers adopt the merchandising philosophy: "Stack it high and watch it fly!" Then you can really spend your time helping customers and not worrying about the little details. Sometimes I think corporate floor plan analysts and company officials spend too much energy on how things look. So much time is spent moving items around that tasks overtake selling as the main priority for associates. Not only does this have an impact on sales, but it also feels like busy-work to the associates and impacts their morale. As an example, I worked for a hard lines retailer whose senior management wanted to provide the customer with a new look every time they entered the store. Figuring regular customers visited the store at least once every two weeks they mandated major floor moves twice a month! So, if we had George Foreman grills in the main aisle at the beginning of the month, we would move them somewhere else in two weeks. Then, because they were such a good seller, we would usually move them *back* into the aisle two weeks after that!! It was so frustrating, because I could have used the time it took to make those two moves to train associates in selling skills or to give extra attention to customers, and there never was any reliable sales data to justify the moves in regard to markedly increased sales.

What's really amazing when considering how much time and effort is spent on how the store looks is that by and large customers don't really seem to notice. A store that seems terribly trashed to a retail professional is just a store to most customers, and while I do advocate keeping a store organized I have felt at times in my career that my sales would have been higher if I could have spent more attention on my customers as opposed to making a fixture look pretty. Have you ever tried to use a floor plan designed by an analyst at corporate who has probably never worked in a store? Just redesigning the plan to fit your store layout can take a huge amount of time! Where do they get some of their ideas anyway? At any rate, there never will be a right answer as to how much time should be spent merchandising as opposed to concentrating on the customer. Suffice it to say that your superiors will expect you to perform both at 100% at all times!

One of the most challenging merchandising endeavors is a new store set-up. That's when a completely empty space must be fixtured and then filled to the brim with product. Depending on the size of the store it can take weeks, even with work going on 24 hours a day. And again, no matter how detailed the fixture plans are, there's always more of some products than the diagram shows and vice versa; that's when merchandising decisions have to be made and there's not a lot of time for figuring it out. Of course, if the night crew does something the managers on the day crew don't like, sometimes whole areas have to be taken apart and redone.

My most tiring new store set-up experience happened about two weeks into a new job. I was immersed in my training to take over the operations manager position at a big-box retailer, and word came that I had been chosen to go to Cincinnati to help with a new store. I drove there that afternoon and checked into a nearby hotel for a two-week stay. When I reported to the store the next morning the store manager informed me that I would be working six days a week and from 8AM-8PM each day. What could I do but just shake my head yes and get to work. It was pretty funny because that manager and his ops manager didn't do any physical work the entire two weeks. They already had their staff because another store in the next town over was closing and everyone was just transferring to the new store. Mostly, they sat in the office and chatted with each other and the several regional managers that had also been brought in—presumably to help. I never saw any of them lift a box or stock a shelf. The most I saw them do was on several occasions they looked at a large display that someone had done and decided that it should be done differently! This really cut deep because if they had just stayed on the floor and helped make merchandising decisions as the product was coming in, a lot of extra work could have been avoided! The worst was when the fire marshall came in to make his final inspection and decided that we had stacked product too close to the ceiling; it was 2PM and he said he'd be back at 4PM and all of it had to be moved. The regionals called all of us together and said we had a grave situation; they told us what we had to do. I'll never forget the reaction I had after I had climbed up a fixture like a monkey and was hurriedly passing product down to the people below and I looked over toward the front doors and saw 5 regional managers standing there watching the rest of us work! It seemed the situation was only grave enough for the lower-level employees to be affected! Even the store manager and his ops were standing there. Ooh, that really sucked!

That reminds me of another phenomenon that occurs during set-ups or when a manager goes to the aid of another manager whose store has gotten a little out of hand. You take time away from your store, travel to the store in question, and immediately start getting treated by the existing staff like a hired hand! Every merchandising suggestion you make is suspect and you're practically afraid to ask for your lunch break. You sort of feel like a second-class citizen even though you are doing a favor. I actually overheard a corporate set-up manager tell a store manager that since the store wasn't open yet no wage and hours officials would be stopping by so therefore they could eliminate the company-mandated break and lunch periods for all the employees working! Every time I do one of these I swear I'll never do another, and then the regional calls and I'm off again.

Hey, speaking of getting product into the store, a really interesting area to discuss concerns the truck drivers who deliver the stuff. Where do I begin? How about the time I ran several small stores and the driver who delivered product to all of them got one of my managers pregnant!! He was only around once a week but they had become friendly and one thing evidently led to another. Well, after the blessed event he transferred to another route and never saw my manager or their baby again. Talk about personal issues affecting work performance!

At another company I worked with a driver who was so friendly, but all the while was robbing the company blind. As all we did was scan the outside label on a shipment box, he made a killing by stealing things out of a box and then resealing it. You know how shipment is, you have to get it the heck inside and then kill yourself to get it on the shelves; you really don't have time to inspect the tape on every box. What eventually ruined his enterprise was a tip from a "friend" of his who evidently wanted to take over the route.

Even the UPS and Fed Ex drivers can cause some angst. Most retailers have an agreement with these companies saying that the driver will deliver the boxes into the store, meaning they are supposed to haul it in the door. Well, some drivers seem to be under the impression that all they have to do is get the stuff out of the truck onto the sidewalk by the door. I have personally hossed huge boxes of stuff into the store because I got tired of waiting for the driver to do something! Let's face it, don't they usually come to the back door with those big, heavy deliveries when you are the only manager on duty and you have to get back on the floor....so, you "help" them.

Chapter 8—The Visit

Every retail manager has had the pleasure of preparing his or her store for a visit from a higher-level company official. At times I suppose this task can be worse than even payroll planning! I like to categorize the visit phenomenon as follows: The visit that never happened; The ugly visit; The okay visit; The to-do list after the visit. All visits cause havoc at the store level. Everything has to be clean and organized. Merchandising must be logical with sales numbers to back it up; this requires the additional step of managers memorizing sales data in case a question is asked about a best and worse seller, etc. Sometimes major floor moves are deemed necessary. And, to top it off, all of this must be accomplished with the previously planned payroll hours—a manager dare not get caught adding precious payroll expense to have all the fixtures dusted—business as usual in terms of helping customers and worst of all a visit from the next level of management to "help" you prepare! This additional visit usually results in a whole extra list of things to do but offers no advice on how to get it done; it's like a dark wind rolls in, exposes everything you've done wrong in the past several months, leaves behind a list of corrections, and then disappears. Many an overnight has been caused by the visit phenomenon, and many hours have been added to a salaried manager's schedule; of course, there's always the promise from the grateful boss that he'll take that into consideration on the next slow day and let you go home early. RIGHT! At any rate, one of the hardest things to do in this situation is to inspire excitement on the part of the regular associates. While a visit can actually make or break an individual manager's career— depending on who is coming— most of the hourly staff could care less! Or, at least they don't feel the same sense of urgency. Regardless, every visit requires an almost superhuman performance by all managers involved, and can lead to some quite volatile emotions.

The Visit That Never Happened—There is nothing worse than killing yourself and getting the staff pumped up only to wait for hours on visit day to no avail! Talk about a morale buster! And yet, every high-level manager I know has had to cancel a scheduled visit for some reason. Now, the reason is probably very important, but to the staff at the store who has worked very hard to prepare, the non-visit probably destroys morale more effectively than any other retail experience. Of course, the store managers try to cover and say that at least the store looks great and isn't everyone proud of all the hard work they've done? But, no matter how much thanks comes from store management, the slight is heavily felt and affects performance beyond visit day. Depending on how many times this happens, it can definitely affect just how motivated a staff is to get ready for the next scheduled visit. I have actually discussed the possibility with several peers that high-level field and corporate officials produce visit schedules periodically that they never intend to follow, just so the stores will get a good cleaning—a forced spring cleaning, if you will. I hope this isn't the case, but in my long career I have experienced many non-visits and nothing has ever topped them in regard to lowering my motivation to perform for my company.

The worst such experience for me was a planned visit from the chairman of the board; at the time I was working for a major national department store and this was a *very* big deal.

For once I had the staff motivated to fever pitch; we had refolded every shirt and pair of denim, sized every 4-way and T-stand, dusted every square inch of floor space and had organized the dock and every stockroom to perfection; I think someone actually ate their lunch off the restroom floor, it was so clean (okay, I'm kidding). Anyway, we were so ready. Since there was no scheduled time of arrival for the important party, we had to keep up everything throughout the day. We were like hawks circling: every time a customer lifted a t shirt off one of our perfectly folded piles we swooped down and refolded it! To the customers we probably looked like crazed escaped convicts; none of us had had enough sleep in the past 3 days and we all had developed nervous ticks from drinking so much coffee to stay awake. As the day wore on we got calls from the stores the party had been to; lots of calls were going back and forth: "Where are they? What time did they leave? What direction did they go? Did they mention where they were going next?" Finally at 6 PM a store 50 miles away said they had just left and were heading back to the airport! We weren't going to get visited after all! Oh the agony! All that work for nothing; oh sure, the store looked great, but how many times do you get to strut your stuff for the chairman of the company? I have never felt more deflated by an event, or a non-event, and all I could do was thank my staff for their hard work. It was pitiful compensation for what they had done. We later learned that when our regional manager picked the chairman up at the airport they had decided on the stores they would actually be able to hit and ours wasn't one of them; apparently the chairman wanted to see some real estate sites that were not near our store. So, the ultimate betrayal was that our regional knew all day they wouldn't be stopping and did not have the decency to call and let us know. I have to admit that something inside me died a little that day; it was a significant piece of my loyalty to my company. A simple phone call—an act of the simplest respect—could have salvaged the situation, but it appeared to all of us at the store that we weren't cared enough about for even that. It wasn't long afterward that I left that job.

The Ugly Visit—If you've ever had one of these you know how bad they are. In fact, fear of one of these happening is probably what motivates most managers to work so hard before a visit! No matter how much preparation has been done, nothing goes right. In my experience the "ugly" visits are usually at the hands of the highest level management visitors. These folks are so elevated in the company that they have forgotten what it is like to run a store—if they ever were at store level to begin with; the worst of them come with an entourage; if they want to make a phone call they turn to the assistant behind them whose job it is to carry the cell phone! I call these types of managers—well, I don't think I can spell that word and remain a lady—anyway, let's just say they have very large egos and have decided that in order to justify their trip away from their cushy office at corporate they must find something very wrong at your store so they can assist you with their vast wisdom! I've actually had one of these guys have someone in his entourage climb a ladder and do the "white glove test" on the top of the fluorescent light fixtures! When this happens you know you are in trouble! It is not uncommon for them to knock down racks, pull stacks of denim out of the walls onto the floor, and release a torrent of comments about your lack of ability right there on the sales floor—in front of associates and customers alike. I have never felt motivated by this "management by fear" technique, but I will admit that I have accepted it as part of the job and humbly agreed with the visitor and promised to do better. Trying to make excuses for whatever I've done incorrectly just makes the situation worse and these aren't the types of folks who accept any back talk. All in all, it is a dismal experience, and after the visitor has left you have to face your associates. Oh yeah, and you have to go around the store and pick up stuff the company leader—in his uncontrollable rage—has left on your sales floor. What a role model! Don't you just want to get promoted so you can act just like that?! If it weren't so serious, you'd have to laugh!

Now, sometimes things at the store just aren't going well and changes need to be made. Usually there are mitigating circumstances: you just took over the store and haven't been able to get it in shape yet; your staff is down with the flu and you've been working with a skeleton crew for the last two weeks; or, you just plain haven't been performing up to par. Unfortunately the "ugly" visitor is not interested in knowing your hardships. If only they could be understanding and just give you pointers it could be such a motivating experience; you're the first to admit when you are not at the top of your game. The visit could be a brainstorming session on how to proceed, a meeting of the minds so to speak, and everyone could leave it enriched in some way. Don't hold your breath. I guess this is why I have never been promoted to that Director of Operations position; my management style is evidently just too "kind and gentle." Surely people will work harder if they are scared to death every time they see someone from corporate!

The Okay Visit—These usually come from the next level of management up—maybe two levels up. These visitors are not so far removed from the stores that they have forgotten the challenge of every day operations and so are more empathetic to performance issues. They still have to get things in shape, but they know that it takes time and effort and will usually concentrate on changes that can be made and not deride the manager on duty. They will recommend merchandising tweaks and will usually give favorable comments on things that pass inspection. After these visits managers usually feel fairly calm, although there is much work to do, and go about making the changes as quickly as they can.

The To-Do-List After The Visit—There's almost always one of these. If you want to really make points, have an associate start to make the changes discussed while the visitor is still there! This shows respect for your visitor and also pegs you as an enthusiastic manager ready to do what it takes. Some retailers actually have visitor logs where all changes to be made are noted and all parties receive a copy; once the store completes the required changes an amended copy is forwarded to the visitor. Whatever the requirements, it behooves the conscientious manager to make the changes quickly and remain outwardly positive while doing so, although sometimes this is hard to do; sometimes you get the feeling it's mostly busy work. After all, if your boss doesn't find something that he can change, what's the use of making a trip out? The main thing is to get through the visit relatively unscathed.

Chapter 9—Let's Get Physical

A retail career is one of the most physical of any careers out there. You know I'm right, but try convincing someone outside the industry! Now, some of the larger square feet stores will have maintenance associates who handle all the daily cleaning and light maintenance work. What a luxury for the managers of those operations! The rest of the retail managers out there must learn to do various tasks related to keeping the store clean and all the equipment functioning. Here's a few examples:

Light bulbs—It sure would be nice if 1) these things would never burn out, and 2) when they do burn out they could change themselves! There's all kinds too—long fluorescent tubes, 5-inch diameter spot lights, huge halogen lights that have a small bulb but have globes that are a square yard in size, etc. I'm not sure which is worse. The fluorescent tubes are very unwieldy and boy is it ever a pain to clean the mess up if you happen to drop one! Oh, one thing that is sure, no matter how clean your store is, the dust on top of one light fixture is enough to make you look like your hair has suddenly turned gray! Because, every bit of whatever dust is on that fixture is going to end up in your hair! You have to be an expert in the use of a very tall ladder—depending how high your ceilings are—and also plan to have a supply of screwdrivers in order to get the old bulbs out.

Garbage—Oh the agony! I hate to take out the garbage at home and there are only two of us. Imagine the amount—and smell—of garbage produced by hundreds of people in the store every day! Probably every manager out there has found something disgusting in the store that had to be thrown out—used condoms or feminine napkins in the fitting rooms, dirty diapers in the restroom trash, etc. Heck, even the garbage can in the employee breakroom can get pretty dicey. Full cups of liquid in the trash can make for lots of excitement when you pull out the bag and it spills on you or all over the floor. Plus, carrying large cardboard boxes from last night's shipment delivery can be treacherous when the wind is blowing at 50 miles per hour and the trash dumpster is 50 feet from the back door! Even if you have a compactor right on your back dock, you still have to lift everything into it and then have to deal with the one-ton load of smashed trash that comes out of it! All in all, this is just one of the worst areas of the job.

Restrooms—This really is the worst area! Where the heck did we put the rubber gloves? Oh, the smells, the sights, the trash. There's just nothing good about having to clean the restrooms. Even being a manager and having the ability to make some poor hourly associate do it doesn't bring any pleasure.

Shelves—Different retailers have different fixturing equipment. Some shelving is metal, some wood. It is all very heavy and unwieldy to maneuver. Usually the shelving material is kept somewhere off the floor and you end up crawling around on the dock or in some dirty back stock room to find not only the right-sized shelves, but also the necessary brackets and hangers. By the time you hoss everything out to the floor you feel like you've run a marathon, and the dumb shelf isn't even up yet. Once you get it into the wall or the fixture—and that's never easy and you hit your finger with the rubber mallot you are using—then you still have to hoss all of the merchandise up onto it. Unfortunately, what was once organized piles when you left to get the shelves is now a mass of mess, because customers have gone through it while you were gone.

Spring Cleaning—Retailers will usually designate at least one period of time a year—sometimes two—for an all-out cleaning of the store. This is where you get to climb up on top of the fixtures and vacuum up the dust that has accumulated there all year. You get to take a screwdriver and try to pry up all the muck that has lodged in the door grates—while you are on your hands and knees doing this you will be asked by every customer who walks past you into the store whether you'd be interested in coming to their house to do windows, etc. You get to wash down all the walls or paint. You'll have to get some putty to fill in the holes in the fitting room walls—bored associates assigned to stay in the fitting room to let customers in will have actually drilled the holes with their keys or pens. Instead of just ordering a new breakroom trash can, you have to hose out the one you have and boy does it ever stink! Obviously, managers are not required to do all these things; however, payroll cuts often occur and sometimes the staff that is there won't do as good a job and it'll have to be done over again.

Gum—It just shows up everywhere—on the floor, in the clothes, on the fixtures, etc. Scraping it off the floor isn't too bad if you have a scraper and can hoist it into the trash bag without having to touch it. There's something about the look of a chewed piece of gum that is just revolting to begin with and having to come into contact with it in any way requires great strength of character. Plus, it's darned hard to remove!

Lions, Tigers and Bears—Well, to be honest, I haven't had to deal with any of these in my store, but there are lots of creepy, crawly things around. The most interesting spiders come in with the shipment boxes! Of course, where there are spiders there can also be snakes and crickets and mice! Dead mice are lots better than live ones. Once I caught a little mouse in the manager's office. Now what do I do? I could have taken him to the pet store next door but they would just have fed him to one of their tarantulas or something. I could have just stepped on him and put him out of my misery. Look, okay, I'm a big animal lover and I just couldn't do either of those. I couldn't put him out the back door because it was just concrete out there. So, I put him in a cup and I drove him to a park down the street; I cried the whole way because it was 10 degrees outside and nothing but snow on the ground; I just knew he'd freeze to death before I could get back to the store! I put him on the ground under a bush and drove off. It was just awful; I came back and told my boss I just didn't think cruelty to animals was in my job description. The only sort of fun thing about little creatures being in the store is to hear the blood-curdling screams of the people who find them; high school girls are just hilarious. Seriously, it really isn't funny and more retailers need to do a better job of keeping their stores free of this type of menace.

Chapter 10—Theft

What can I say? This is one of the most disgusting areas of retail management. Whether associate theft, customer theft, or vendor theft, it is unfortunately something that every manager is forced to deal with. Studies by loss prevention consultants show that associate theft causes the majority of store shrink. When I first started in retail there used to be a common saying which I'm sure is still true to this day: "Of all the people out there, five percent will never steal, five percent will steal every chance they get, and the other 90 % will not ordinarily steal, but if it is made very easy for them to do so, they might." That's a pretty large number of your associates, customers and vendors that might steal from you if you let your guard down. Of course, the difficult thing is, how do you do everything you are supposed to do and still have time to keep an eye on everyone?!

Cash shortage is the easiest to detect. When the day is closed you know what you should be depositing and any differences are immediately apparent. The best way to avoid cash shortages, or at least allow you to identify possible thieves quickly is to have each cash drawer assigned to only one cashier. That's easier said than done these days, especially with the push to increase the speed at checkout. Some major retailers have gone to a system where they have several registers loaded with drawers and when lines get long a multitude of associates are called off the sales floor to ring; naturally, these drawers are the ones that fall short the most. Unfortunately, even though associates are assigned a cashier number to use it is still impossible to blame any one cashier for shortage on a drawer that has been used by up to five or six people. The best you can do is track drawer shortage by all cashiers involved and observe any trends. Over the last several years I have noticed a relaxing of cash shortage policies by most retailers. I used to have to report to the next level a cash shortage of $10 or more; now it seems as though $50 is the level at which most retailers want store management to report to loss prevention or regional managers. Evidently, some cash shortage is acceptable as long as customer service remains the priority.

Inventory shrink is often shocking. It is impossible to keep track of every item on the floor and even in the smallest of stores an amazing amount of merchandise can go missing between inventory audits. This is the hardest theft to deter and to catch. Simple techniques include inspecting associate belongings upon their departure from the premises, having associate purchases rung out by store management or cashiers with elevated status and confirming the number of packages delivered with a vendor bill of lading. Some retailers pay loss prevention staffs to watch the floor; sophisticated camera equipment can scan every area of the floor and registers can send real time item scanning data to the loss prevention office as the customer is being rung out. Sensors attached to apparel are common deterrents although most can be breached by professional thieves. All these attempts to thwart theft are very expensive and result in higher product costs for consumers.

While theft is a common bane to the retail manager, it never ceases to amaze me the lengths some folks go to in order to steal. Once I was on the floor when my store's LP guy caught a woman concealing some jewelry. He took her into his office and as was policy asked me to accompany them so that he was not alone with the alleged perpetrator. He told her to give up everything she had taken and as he walked out of the room he said, "I want that girdle too." As I sat there amazed, she pulled up her skirt and pulled down the girdle and out popped four men's dress shirts and a pair of slacks!

She was just a little slip of a thing and it would not have occurred to anyone without a trained eye that she was concealing over $250 worth of merchandise under her skirt! Of course, it was rather uncomfortable for me to sit there while she disrobed and pleaded with me not to let the LP guy call the police; according to her, she was stealing so that she could buy her teenage daughter a dress for her prom. It turned out that she was high on some kind of drugs and the police came and took her away.

While it is uncomfortable to be a part of an apprehension, it is also very exciting. Even though LP issues are supposed to be top secret, every associate knows when an apprehension is going down; the buzz is all over the store in minutes! It's like, "Score one for the good guys!" Another case I can recall involved an associate whose apartment had suddenly become furnished with hard line items from my store; I was tipped off to this fact by the associate's girlfriend who also worked for me; I still scratch my head regarding the type of relationship they must have shared? At any rate, the girlfriend told me one day that some of the associate's friends were in the store and that they were buying some things. When they were being checked out I went to the register and saw that they were purchasing a lamp, which came packaged in a large box. Using the excuse that we had been having trouble with the manufacturer not sending the lamps pictured on the boxes, I opened the box and found not only the lamp but also a clock, electric shaver and an expensive knife set—about $300 worth of merchandise. The associate in question would have had to retrieve the box from the stockroom and he was actually standing beside his friends as they were checking out. All of them were detained, but since the friends pleaded no knowledge and had not walked out of the building with the merchandise, they were let go. The associate, however, left the building in handcuffs and all his fellow associates saw him go. This young man was going to college and came from a very good family. He didn't really need the items but because it was easy to beat the system he did so. I was so disillusioned, as I always am when a young person betrays me, but he will have to deal with his mistake for the rest of his life.

One time I was closing a register and noticed that a doll that had been placed on the register lane as an impulse item was not sitting up straight. When I took hold of it to right it I felt something under its dress. Hey, a manager has got to do what a manger has got to do...I undressed the doll and found a crisp $50 bill inside its clothes. Sure enough, when I counted the drawer down it was exactly $50 short. Had I not found the money, the cashier who had put it there would have picked it up the next time she worked. As it was, several people had rung on the drawer that day so we never did find out who did it.

Another example of employee theft is this one. A store I was sent in to trouble-shoot was having massive inventory shrink. There was just no way customers were getting it all so I spent a lot of time observing the habits of the associates. Eventually I noticed that two of the assistant managers were spending an inordinate amount of time in the ladies rest room. Finally one day I went in there and just leaned on one of the sinks to ponder their attraction to the room. I looked up and saw that one of the ceiling tiles was askew. I climbed up on the toilet seat and pushed it aside and found a huge bundle of company product up there!! There's no telling how long they had been stealing things by putting it up there and then having their friends come in and put it in shopping bags they had entered the store with and walk out the door. Now every time I go to work for a new retailer I check for ceiling tiles in the rest rooms and offices!!

Other frustrating types of theft for me are shoplifting incidents that I can't do anything about. One day a customer came to me and said that she had seen a man stuffing items under his ski jacket. As she was telling me this the guy was heading toward the front door, so I ran over there. His coat was so full of stuff that he could not put his arms down, but because I had not seen him conceal the items I could not stop him; the company I was working for at the time had no LP staff and managers were forbidden to make a stop unless they had seen everything! Boy, was that a frustrating job, because evidently all the thieves knew the policy too and we were sitting ducks. But, the company was so afraid of lawsuits resulting from bad stops that it budgeted a percentage of sales for theft and did not want shoplifters apprehended unless several criteria were met.

In fact, most retailers—for the same reason—do not advocate that their employees get involved unless they are 100% sure a theft has taken place. Bad stops—where an employee makes an accusation of theft against someone who is eventually proven to be innocent—have led to serious lawsuits for retailers and loss of employment for those involved. The days of an associate running down the mall after a shoplifter are hopefully behind us; it's just too dangerous. Thankfully, in the case of armed robbery, all retailers train their employees to give the robbers whatever they ask for without attempting any retaliation on behalf of the store's property. Associates who have successfully thwarted a robbery despite the policy are usually fired anyway—causing huge media coverage and consumer outrage—so it behooves most retail employees to mind their own business where theft is concerned. It's difficult, though, when you've worked and sweat to make the store look good and someone can violate it so easily with seemingly no consequences. I think managers and associates alike have felt frustration and rage at this all too common phenomenon.

Chapter 11—Stupid Things Bosses Say

This chapter is mostly for shock value. Although, I would venture to say that some of these lines will be quite similar to ones you've heard over the years.

"Well, you seem to be the only manager having trouble implementing the new program." This remark is always made by a multi-unit manager when you tell him the new policy or program from corporate is difficult to administer. It doesn't matter if *every one* of his stores is having trouble with it, he will always try to make you feel you are the only one. My advice is to call other stores before you complain to the next level.

"Those of you who posted a bad inventory figure better spread your cheeks, because when the VP visits next week, he's going to want to share some love." I swear to you this remark was actually made on a conference call by a regional manager! The company was a national chain and the conference call was a weekly requirement for all GM's and Ops managers. I was horrified, but when I complained to my GM that I thought the remark was highly inflammatory, he just said "What can I do, the guy is my boss?" I actually went to HR on this one, but because this remark was fine based on the culture at that particular company, my HR rep actually laughed at me when I complained about it. I must admit that after I left the company I was not surprised to see that they were having major turnover and financial problems.

"Now, we do pretty well as far as customer service goes. Of course we can always do better. I guess I'd have to say that in this area we could be described as tall midgets." This remark was made by the Chairman of a national retailer on the "Welcome to the company" video that was required viewing for every new employee!

"Rodents are fairly routine in retail. Just call maintenance." This remark was made to me by a regional manager after I told her we had mouse droppings all over the sales floor and had just found a live mouse in the pant leg of a pair of slacks we were moving to another area on the floor. As the problem got worse I wrote her a memo telling her that as I was writing it I had to have my feet on the chair in the manager's office because mice were actually running back and forth across the floor. I wrote her several subsequent memos to inform her we were finding dead mice in the stock rooms and on the floor, and that the odor of dead mice in the walls of the manager's office was making all the managers sick. The regional never visited the store to assess the problem, she did not call anyone at corporate to speed the handling of the problem, and she never once called the store about whether the problem was being solved.

"This company wants their managers to bonus at least 50% of the time." A regional manager told me this while she was trying to recruit me. I told her that I'd rather she pay me higher up front in salary. I eventually took the job, stayed with the company about 2 ½ years and made bonus about 5 times! For heaven's sake, don't fall for this one!!

"Within two hours I need you to project sales and payroll for January, February and March." This wouldn't be so bad, except that it was August and I was right in the middle of the Back-To-School sales phenomenon! That year I was comping at 120% every day and believe me, the furthest thing from my mind was what I might do five months down the line.

"We can't fire him for that offense unless you have him on a final written warning for the same activity." Nowadays, with lawsuits running rampant, terminating someone—even for just cause—has become one of the hardest things for a manager to do. I wanted to fire a subordinate manager and naturally needed my regional's permission. The manager had been caught throwing an hourly associate—a minor who had just had a cast removed from his arm—to the floor and holding him down. Both the manager and the associate said that it was just horseplay but it was done in front of other employees and was specifically noted in the policy manual as a reason for termination. I told my regional that I would never again feel comfortable having this manager making decisions affecting my store, especially since he opened and closed many times a week without me there. Instead of firing him my regional moved him to another store—the one he had been wanting to go to anyway since it was closer to his home; I swear there's nothing like being rewarded for bad behavior.

"I wasn't aware they did that type of surgery this time of year." Remember this one from my regional when I told her I might have to be off during the holiday season due to having a tumor removed?

Chapter 12—Miscellaneous Retail Fun

Here's just a few things that weren't grandiose enough to warrant their own chapters, but make the retail life what it is just the same.

In the ladies room, you need to post a sign that says: "Please remain seated until the performance is over." You'll never get it approved, but wouldn't it help immensely?

Nine times out of ten, people who are really sick call the manager themselves to say they can't work their shift. Otherwise, you get the call from parents, spouses, roommates, etc.

Sooner or later you will have to plunge a stopped-up toilet or help clean up the most god-awful mess in the restroom. That's when you know you need the sign mentioned above.

If you are having trouble selling an item, park a ladder beside it, climb up on the ladder and try to look busy.

Within seconds, every customer in the store will be drawn to you like steel to a magnet!

Be prepared to be standing beside a customer in front of the registers and have the customer ask you "Where do I check out?"

There's always a love-hate relationship between same-company stores in close proximity to each other. You need them to provide quick availability for items you don't have on hand, but…they never answer the phone fast enough, and their associates never know what they are doing, and they never follow company directives correctly, whereas you do, and customers will always come to your store and complain about them. Think about the closest store to you, the one you've called so much you've memorized the number. Am I right?

Associates have this unexplainable need to discuss the sexual needs of their managers. If you are cranky all the time, you can bet they've discussed a cure for you!

No matter how many associates are on staff, the associate breakroom on any given day looks like animals have overrun it. You find yourself wondering why people can't clean up after themselves. It seems so simple.

When you order writing pens, order 5 times more than you think you could ever go through! No matter how many you have on hand, you will never be able to find one when you need to sign something.

Be prepared to find unexplainable bruises on every part of your body.

Despite the fact that you have been dead all evening, you will always have hangers-on at closing time. Why can't these people read your posted hours? They are so insensitive to the fact that it takes an extra hour to get out of there after the last customer leaves.

At some point, after it has caused you much angst, you will finally receive and understand the revelation that hourly associates will never care about what happens at the store as much as you do. The more you try to prove this theory wrong, the more trouble you will have.

Retail people naturally walk faster than most people. If a customer asks you where something is and you tell them you'll take them there, be prepared to turn around after a few steps and see that they are far behind you struggling to keep up. I have actually clocked myself at 3.5 mph without even trying to walk fast!

Retail is the original "incestuous" industry. So many longtime retail professionals have worked for so many different companies that sometimes it seems that everyone you know has worked with everyone else you know at one time or another. It's actually fairly easy for a good manager to change companies and it is so common that most retailers don't worry about hiring someone with several job changes on their resume.

If you are doing any routine cleaning projects at your store, be prepared to be asked by 90% of the customers that pass by you whether you do windows.

You'll be out shopping at another store with your family and you will suddenly find yourself folding a t shirt on a sloppy table, or hanging an item on an empty t-stand arm so no one hits their head. It's the "recovery disease" and every manager gets it.

Another definition for "conference call" is "useless waste of time."

The store floor plan sent out by corporate—the one that tells you where to put everything—never fits your store.

You could sure get a lot more projects done if customers didn't keep bothering you.

Whatever they tell you about training in the interview—forget it. For the most part you'll have to train yourself once you get in the position. If they show you a big training manual, just smile and pretend that you believe them; actually, a lot of those recruiters don't know that the manual is really just a "dog and pony" show to entice prospective management candidates into thinking that they'll get fully trained before taking on any responsibility.

What was that buyer thinking?

Customers only hear what they want to in regard to promotions. One or more will always try to extend the deadline or get a better deal than the ad says.

Why won't those window signs ever stay up? Where does the distribution center get those suction cups anyway? They never work!

200 units processed per man hour?! Can the Vice President of Store Operations process 200 units per hour? I'd like to see a video of that!

The Vice President of Store Operations probably couldn't ring a customer's purchase up if his life depended on it. Heck, the guy from my current company won't even carry his own cell phone!

Why does there have to be trash?!

Sooner or later you will have to take your ring to the jewelers. Because of the shape it is in, be prepared for the jeweler to ask you if you work construction.

Associates who complain the worst when hours are cut during slow times are the ones most likely to turn down added shifts.

One of the most favorite topics of associates: What do those managers do in that office?

No matter how prepared you think you are in terms of staffing for markdowns, shipment deliveries, floor moves, inventory, etc., something always comes up. Either you have an hourly associate call off, or your partner manager comes down with "pink eye" or a toothache. Being just one person shy of the original plan can cause major havoc and completely throw off the rest of the day!!

When you finally admit that you are deathly ill and have to go home early, a call to let your boss know will always garner the same question: "Did you cover the store?" It's like, "Da, of course I covered it or I wouldn't be leaving!"

Chapter 13—Intrigue (or The Rumor Mill)

I don't know why it is, but retail is rife with intrigue. You'd think that associates would have so much to do that they would have little time to gossip. Not so. It seems there is no end to fodder for debate and no time like the present to explore it.

Unfortunately, managers tend to be the subject of much of this conversation. A variety of issues prevail. Appearance is discussed at length. Perhaps a manager has put on a little weight recently. Could it be because the person in question is spending too much time in the manager's office and not enough on the floor? What about a slow metabolism caused by depression over an ended relationship? Or, did you see what she eats every day at lunch; you can't eat all those fried foods and stay thin, even in retail! Now, why any of this would be of interest to associates is beyond my comprehension, but it always seems to be very important to some of them.

Probably the most common issue discussed is a manager's relationship status. Are they married? (Who could live with a bitch like her?); Are they dating? (I saw them at a bar the other night and boy was he a dog!); Are they gay or straight? (He never talks about a girlfriend!) A manager's home life is at the root of many an amateur psychologist's explanation of in-store behavior. (Well, you know she has a lousy marriage, which is why she takes out all her frustrations on us!); (Wouldn't you be crabby if you hadn't had sex in 20 years?); (Boy, she's in a good mood today, guess we all know what happened last night!).

Another provider of on-the-job entertainment is the ever-popular game: "Pit the managers against each other." This is accomplished when more worldly and experienced associates detect a less than optimal working relationship between two managers. While one is away someone says to the other one, "Do you know what so-and-so said about you the other day?" Now, most managers know this is a trap, but sometimes the rigors of retail are so draining that even the most hardened manager lets his or her guard down. Once they ask for details the game is off and away. Soon the other manager is similarly baited and the fun ensues. Well, fun for the associates, that is. The managers involved are now stuck in an uncomfortable cycle of analyzing every comment and re-thinking past actions for ulterior motives. The associates who started it all watch from the sidelines. Why would they do it? Perhaps low pay, lousy hours and physically challenging work have something to do with the need for entertainment. The only thing that can rectify this situation is a heart-to-heart between the managers in question, usually preceded by a last straw sort of comment and a preparation for coming to blows. Afterwards, the managers swear never to trust the associates again and don't...until the rigors of retail cause them to drop their guard again.

Rest assured that all associates somehow find out when a manager is in hot water with the boss! Whether it's a merchandising issue—heck, they work your area and know when it's not organized—or something to do with a missed promotion opportunity, it seems everyone knows about it. Shortages at the store, both cash and inventory, lead to lots of discussion by associates and managers alike. Of course, shortages are supposed to be kept hush-hush, but somehow everyone eventually knows about them. Rumors about who is stealing can take on unbelievable proportions, and no one is safe. It's even gamier when a representative from corporate loss prevention gets involved and interviews several people or the entire staff! Sales activity on the floor during these times is at an all-time low; staff reaction encompasses everything from curiosity about what everyone else got asked, to indignation about being interviewed in the first place. Suffice it to say that rumors regarding the integrity, or lack thereof, of anyone on the staff, can have quite a negative impact on day-to-day retail operations. And, while it is up to management to squelch them, it is difficult to do so given the enormity of the task.

Another fun area of debate is how long a manager will last; either they leave the company of their own accord or they are made to exit. We bring this type of gossip on ourselves I think. I don't know a manager out there who hasn't said at one time or another within earshot of an associate, "I swear I'm going to update my resume and start looking for another job!" Usually it is said during times of extreme frustration and not really meant for general consumption, but once said the employees take it as gospel and not only are the bets on, but they manage to tell just about everyone they come into contact with! This can be a potentially negative situation if the higher-ups get wind of it. Any thoughts they might have had about the manager in question's upward mobility will usually be cast aside— why waste time on someone bound and determined to leave the company? I made the mistake once, out of respect and friendship for my boss, of telling her I was looking around in hopes of leaving retail altogether; I honestly said I didn't really have anything in the works yet and that I did not want the regional to know about my plans. How naïve I was! My boss, obviously no longer a friend, turned right around and called the regional! It wouldn't have been so bad except that the job I wanted wasn't going to be available for over a year and in the meantime I wanted to take on more responsibility at my current company. Well, I was totally taken off any list for promotion opportunities; not only did I lose money, but the company lost the contribution I could have made at a higher level. I was absolutely trapped where I was, and even if I had decided to stay with the company, I was without an avenue to progress! Believe me, this made my remaining time with the company less than motivated!

Chapter 14—Fun With Customers

"Do you work here?" This question will be asked at various times:
—when you are fully dressed in your store uniform,
—when you are up on a ladder placing stock
—when you are on your hands and knees building a shelf
—when you are standing at a register

"Where's the bathroom?" I once had so many customers asking my associates this question that I requested a sign to be erected which pointed out the direction of the rest rooms; my regional manager refused the request, saying that we didn't have signs like that because the company didn't really want the customers to know that we had rest rooms!

"What size do I wear?" This question is usually accompanied by a request to look in the back of a customer's pants to see what size they actually have on! Oh the agony!

Some customers will tell you their life story on the phone, which wouldn't be so bad if you weren't in the middle of ringing the register with three people standing behind you waiting to ask you a question.

A "Closing" Scenario: The store has just closed. The front doors are locked. You are inside stocking a new item. A customer comes to one of the doors and tries it. When that one is locked, they try the other one. When that one is locked, they look at the store hours posted on the window. They look at their watch. They look at you. They try the first door again. They look at you again and knock. You mouth, "closed" and point to your watch. They stare at you for a minute. They try the first door again. You say something under your breath!

Customers with young children in tow always leave behind the most interesting foodstuffs: Cheerios in the shopping cart; Gummi bears in the dressing room; a trail of squashed raisons all over the sales floor. Once I saw a little kid crawling around on the floor—turned out he was eating small pieces of candy dropped there the night before by another kid! Pepto Bismol anyone!!

Younger customers seem to be addicted to doors and mirrors. They absolutely have to touch them, and the stickier their hands, the better!

It is amazing how cavalier many customers are with their car and house keys. I've found sets in the fitting room, on the cashwrap, mixed in clothing on a table, in the restrooms, inside outerwear pockets, etc. The worst is when they lose them near closing time and your whole routine is thrown off because everyone is helping them look!

Let's face it, some customers are just plain mean. Many's the time I've had to console a teary-eyed cashier, telling her to "shake it off, it wasn't personal" but it sure seems like it at the time. As a manager, I feel it is my responsibility to protect my associates and provide them with a pleasant working environment; when it comes to rude customers I have actually asked them to act with a little more decorum, and if that hasn't worked, to leave the store—sometimes under police escort depending on how bad they get—if they did not treat my employees with respect.

Some customers just have to tell you what's on their mind. The other day a customer said to my cashier,

"Well, I've been to 3 of your stores today, and I'd have to say that this one has been the messiest. I just can't understand that." Obviously, if the store is messy, there must be mitigating circumstances, like no payroll, call-offs, etc. I know the customer's perception is important, but why do some of them have to make it their business to tell you something you already know and are trying so hard to remedy?

Chapter 15—Do I Really Want To Stay In Retail?

Who among us has **never** asked this question? Oh, to have a job where I know my schedule months in advance...better yet, how about Monday through Friday with every weekend off? How do you even go about trying to break out of the industry? Sure, any retailer will hire a manger worth his or her salt, but how do you convince Corporate America that you have skills that are transferable to an office setting? If you stay in retail for any length of time you can usually get yourself to a pretty impressive salary and bonus level. To start out in a totally different industry sometimes requires a pay cut in addition to loss of autonomy. Then there's the issue of which, if any, industries look at retail as a good stepping stone. I have found that most banking institutions appreciate the customer service skills of former retail employees.

However, most corporate recruiters or headhunters cannot squeeze the retail experience into a small enough niche for their purposes. How do you define what it is that you are so good at doing? You're good at quite a few things—sales, recruiting, inventory control, facility maintenance, cash control, training, financial analysis, budgeting and planning, etc. Heck, you can even paint and repair broken equipment! It's sort of hard to narrow down and even harder to convince a non-retail professional to look at your resume in regard to a search for a specific job title. For instance, Human Resource jobs are hard to come by even though retail managers deal with a wide range of HR issues on a daily basis; when applying for an HR job, the title "HR Manager" or "HR Generalist" is missing from a store manager's resume, and though they've done the work, the screening process oftentimes keys in on the lack of these titles and the resume is put into the "do not contact" file—especially now that many firms are using "key word" software programs to screen the resumes of prospective candidates. I actually had a hiring manager say to me in an interview—after I had explained to him I had 20 years of Retail Management experience—"It's just a shame you don't have any HR experience." I just about fell off my chair, but then I figured it just proved what I'm trying to get across in this chapter. In the same vein, being taken seriously when applying for a "trainer" position at a manufacturing company is difficult because recruiters for manufacturing companies will generally want to talk to someone who has been basically...*a trainer*—preferably in the manufacturing industry. Don't ask me why this is so. You don't have "Trainer" listed as one of your jobs because training was only a *part* of your position titled "Store Manager." I truly believe that someone who has never been in retail has no idea how well rounded retail managers have to be and to them "Store Manager" on a resume means someone who can *only* work at a store where products are sold, whatever they think that entails. They don't look at the individual skills the retail manager has and thus will not normally think of them in regard to filling a staff position in HR or accounting or training. A headhunter once explained to me that the firms he deals with use him because he will get them a person who has done a specific job; remember that companies pay these guys lots of money, so they are not going to jeopardize their working relationship with the client by sending folks that don't fit the *exact* description.

All in all, it's pretty hard for an established retail manager who wants to remain at a certain salary level to go anywhere but to another retail company. Usually you can parlay your experience into more money and a higher level of merchandising or operations responsibility. But, you still have the holiday and scheduling issues to contend with. At least the higher you go the more control you have over your personal schedule.

One thing that can certainly be said about a career in retail is this: if you work hard and keep out of trouble, and your company is strong, you usually are pretty secure in your job. Even if your company goes under, there's usually lots of other retailers out there looking for good managers. Of course, with the recent industry sales slump, many retailers are curbing planned growth and a large number have had to close stores that are not performing. While the number of managers out there looking for retail jobs has increased in the last few months, it is still possible for strong performers to find positions with the stronger companies. In that way, retail management is sometimes a much more secure profession than say, a staff scientist or analyst in a manufacturing company; if you get laid off the latter, it might be very difficult to find a similar job right away, especially if the industry is in a downturn situation; for the former, a comparative job could probably be obtained within a week or two; if a retail position is hard to find, you can easily parlay your experience into a job in another service industry—food, hospitality, etc. You can bring immediate sales results to your company on day one and that is a very powerful skill to market.

Besides, what other profession can offer you the excitement of a new crisis to deal with every day? If it's not a leaking roof, it's a sexual harassment issue between two of your associates. If you've been in retail for any length of time, there probably isn't anything that could happen that would shock you or throw you off track. You can break sales records on a shoestring budget and do it with panache. You can fix anything and do whatever it takes to get the job done, even if it means *you* clean the restrooms today! Not every professional manager can promise that much commitment. At the very least, take pride in the fact that you regularly rise to any occasion and can wear many hats every day. That's retail folks!! Might as well be proud of yourself while you are here!!

POSTSCRIPT

Well, I finally gave up trying to look for another job while still in the clutches of retail. I quit my retail job a few months ago. Despite the financial considerations I have never been happier! I feel so free and relieved. I haven't been sick either—not even a cold!! I suppose the amazing metamorphosis I have experienced since leaving the field means that I probably was never suited for retail in the first place. Although, for many years I made a good living and certainly added to the prosperity of the companies for which I worked.

Since leaving I have actually enjoyed going into stores. I find myself relating to the pained looks on associates' and managers' faces and many times I've said in an empathetic tone, "I used to be in retail too, so I know what you are going through." The fact that someone understands whatever problem they are having seems to calm them and I usually leave feeling like I've helped a former colleague through a rough time, or at least provided a small bright spot in an otherwise stressful day.

I am at peace now, but will hold my retail experiences close to my heart for one reason: they remind me that I can do anything the situation calls for and be successful at it!! Few people know that about themselves.

0-595-22496-2